Mom's One Line a 1

A THREE-YEAR MEMORY BOOK

Diana Lynn

Published by D&D Graphics in 2018
First edition; First printing

Design and writing © 2018 Diana Lynn

ISBN 978-1-947594-01-2

This journal belongs to:

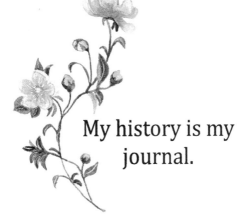

My history is my journal.

How to use this journal

This journal is created for a 3 year span with each page having room for one or two lines of writing per year. Simply fill in the year behind the 20 and you're ready to start.

As you fill in the current date you'll have a wonderful reminder of what you did, or what happened on that exact date! At the end of each month there are lined pages for additonal thoughts.

There's no reason to wait until January 1st, just start right away!

These types of journals make great family keepsakes that can be treasured and passed down to your children and grand-children.

IF FOUND, PLEASE RETURN TO:

NAME

ADDRESS

PHONE

EMAIL

 # JANUARY

1

(20)

(20)

(20)

JANUARY

2

(20)

(20)

(20)

JANUARY
3

20

20

20

 # JANUARY
4

20

20

20

JANUARY
5

20

20

20

 # JANUARY

6

 20

20

20

JANUARY
7

20

20

20

 # JANUARY
8

20 ⬭

20 ⬭

20 ⬭

 # JANUARY
9

20

20

20

JANUARY
10

20

20

20

 # JANUARY
11

20

20

20

 # JANUARY
12

(20)

(20)

(20)

JANUARY
13

20

20

20

 # JANUARY
14

(20)

(20)

(20)

JANUARY
15

$\left(\ 20\ \right)$

$\left(\ 20\ \right)$

$\left(\ 20\ \right)$

 # JANUARY
16

(20)

(20)

(20)

 # JANUARY
17

20

20

20

JANUARY
18

20

20

20

# JANUARY
19

(20)

(20)

(20)

JANUARY

20

(20)

(20)

(20)

 # JANUARY
21

(20)

(20)

(20)

JANUARY
22

20

20

20

 # JANUARY
23

20

20

20

JANUARY
24

20

20

20

JANUARY
25

20

20

20

JANUARY
26

20

20

20

JANUARY
27

20

20

20

JANUARY
28

20

20

20

JANUARY
29

20

20

20

 # JANUARY
30

$\big(\,20\,\big)$

$\big(\,20\,\big)$

$\big(\,20\,\big)$

JANUARY
31

20

20

20

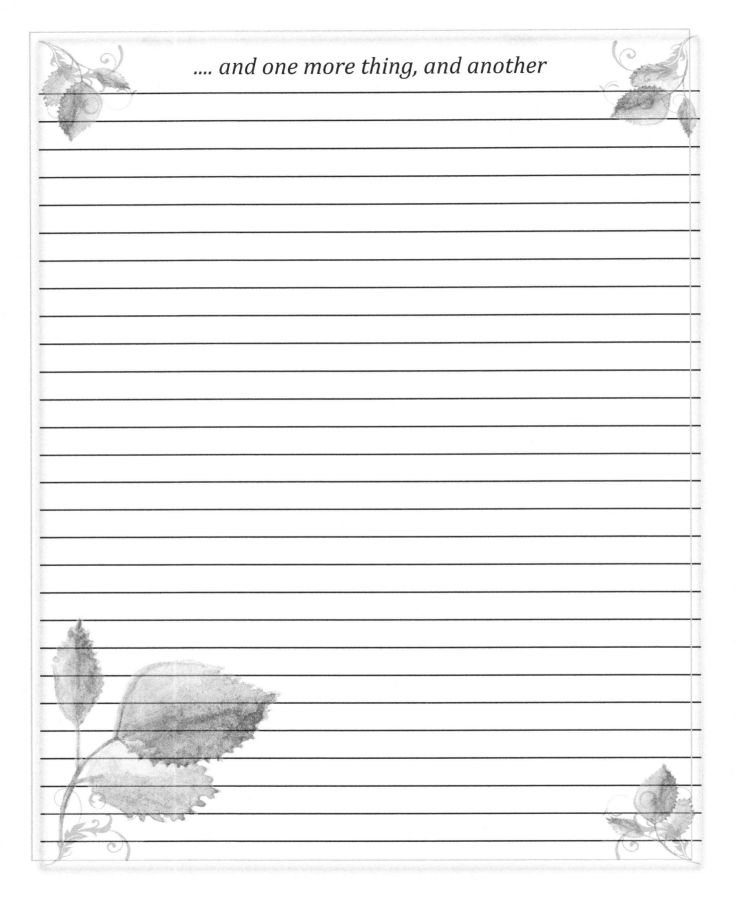

.... and one more thing, and another

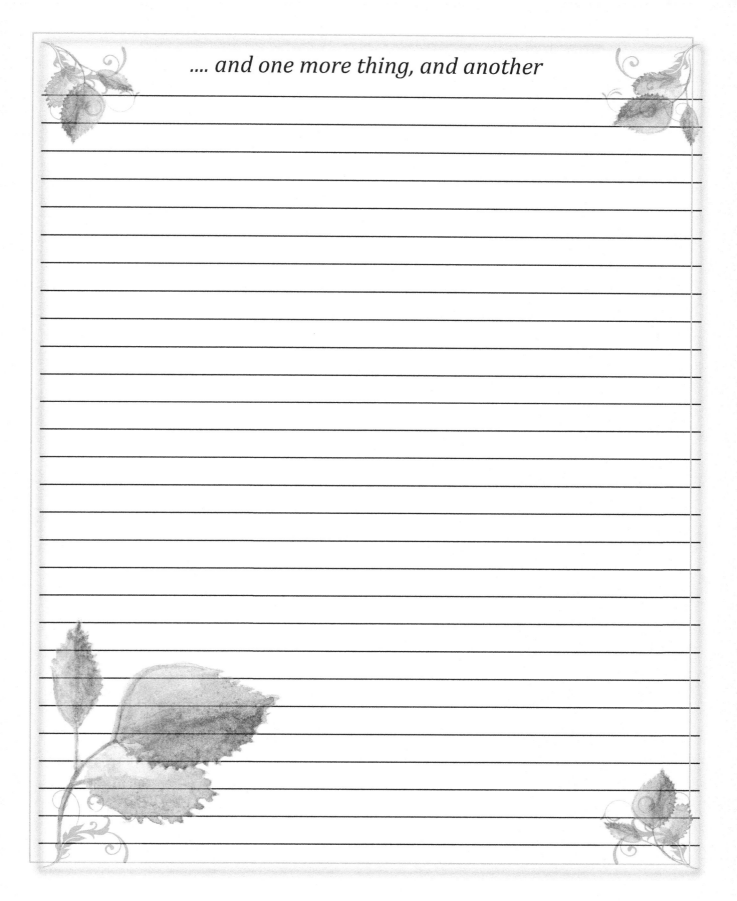

.... and one more thing, and another

.... and one more thing, and another

FEBRUARY

1

20

20

20

 # FEBRUARY
2

$\Big(\!$ 20 $\!\Big)$

$\Big(\!$ 20 $\!\Big)$

$\Big(\!$ 20 $\!\Big)$

 # FEBRUARY

3

Mom's One Line a Day by Diana Lynn Copyright © 2018 D &D Graphics

FEBRUARY
4

20

20

20

FEBRUARY
5

20

20

20

FEBRUARY
6

$\boxed{20}$

$\boxed{20}$

$\boxed{20}$

 # FEBRUARY
7

20

20

20

 # FEBRUARY

8

20

20

20

 # FEBRUARY

9

20

20

20

FEBRUARY
10

20

20

20

 # FEBRUARY

11

20

20

20

 # FEBRUARY
12

20

20

20

 # FEBRUARY
13

$\left(\,20\quad\right)$

$\left(\,20\quad\right)$

$\left(\,20\quad\right)$

FEBRUARY
14

20

20

20

FEBRUARY
15

20

20

20

 # FEBRUARY
16

(20)

(20)

(20)

 # FEBRUARY
17

20

20

20

 # FEBRUARY
18

$\left(\ 20\ \right)$

$\left(\ 20\ \right)$

$\left(\ 20\ \right)$

FEBRUARY
19

20

20

20

FEBRUARY

20

20

20

20

 # FEBRUARY

21

20

20

20

FEBRUARY
22

 # FEBRUARY

23

20

20

20

 # FEBRUARY
24

20

20

20

FEBRUARY
25

20

20

20

 # FEBRUARY

26

20

20

20

# FEBRUARY
27

20

20

20

 # FEBRUARY
28

20

20

20

 # FEBRUARY
29

20

20

20

.... and one more thing, and another

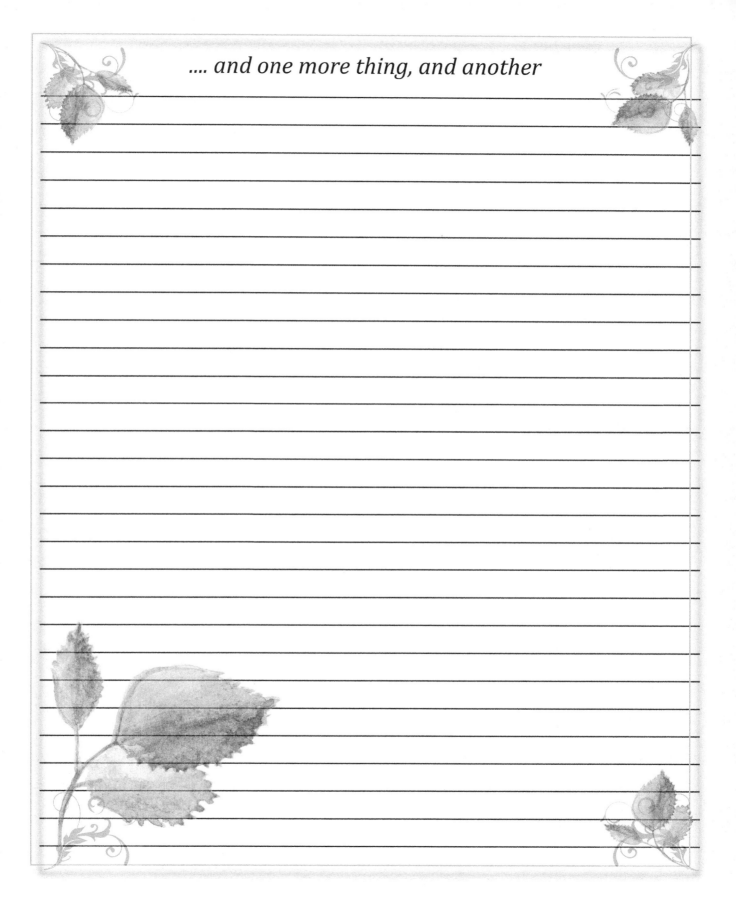

.... and one more thing, and another

.... and one more thing, and another

MARCH
1

(20)

(20)

(20)

MARCH
2

20

20

20

MARCH
3

20

20

20

MARCH
4

20

20

20

MARCH
5

20

20

20

 # MARCH

6

(20)

(20)

(20)

 # MARCH
7

20

20

20

MARCH
8

20

20

20

MARCH
9

20

20

20

MARCH
10

20

20

20

MARCH
11

20

20

20

 # MARCH
12

$\big($ 20 $\big)$

$\big($ 20 $\big)$

$\big($ 20 $\big)$

MARCH
13

20

20

20

 # MARCH
14

(20)

(20)

(20)

 # MARCH

15

20

20

20

 # MARCH

16

(20)

(20)

(20)

MARCH
17

20

20

20

 # MARCH
18

20

20

20

MARCH
19

(20)

(20)

(20)

MARCH
20

(20)

(20)

(20)

MARCH
21

20

20

20

MARCH
22

20

20

20

MARCH
23

20

20

20

MARCH
24

$\boxed{20}$

$\boxed{20}$

$\boxed{20}$

MARCH
25

20

20

20

MARCH
26

(20)

(20)

(20)

 # MARCH
27

20

20

20

 # MARCH
28

20

20

20

MARCH
29

20

20

20

MARCH
30

20

20

20

MARCH
31

20

20

20

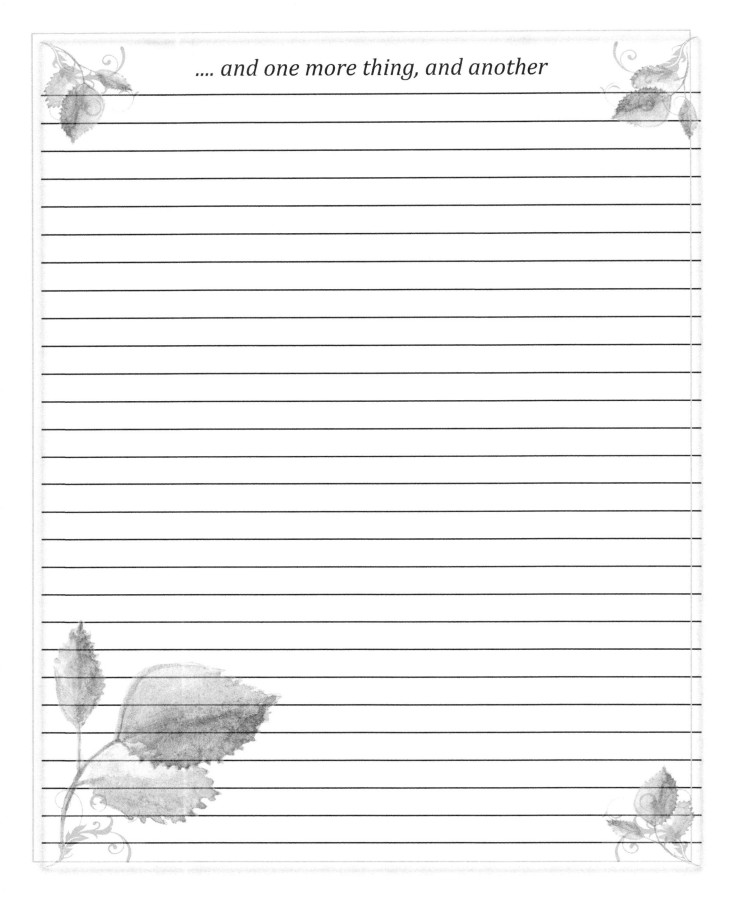

.... and one more thing, and another

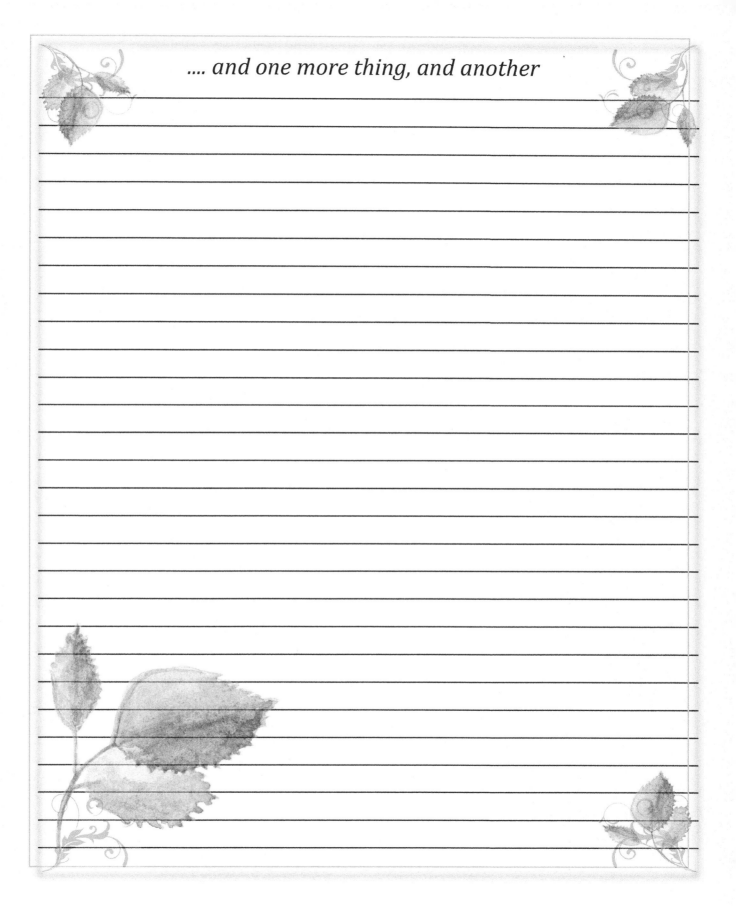

.... and one more thing, and another

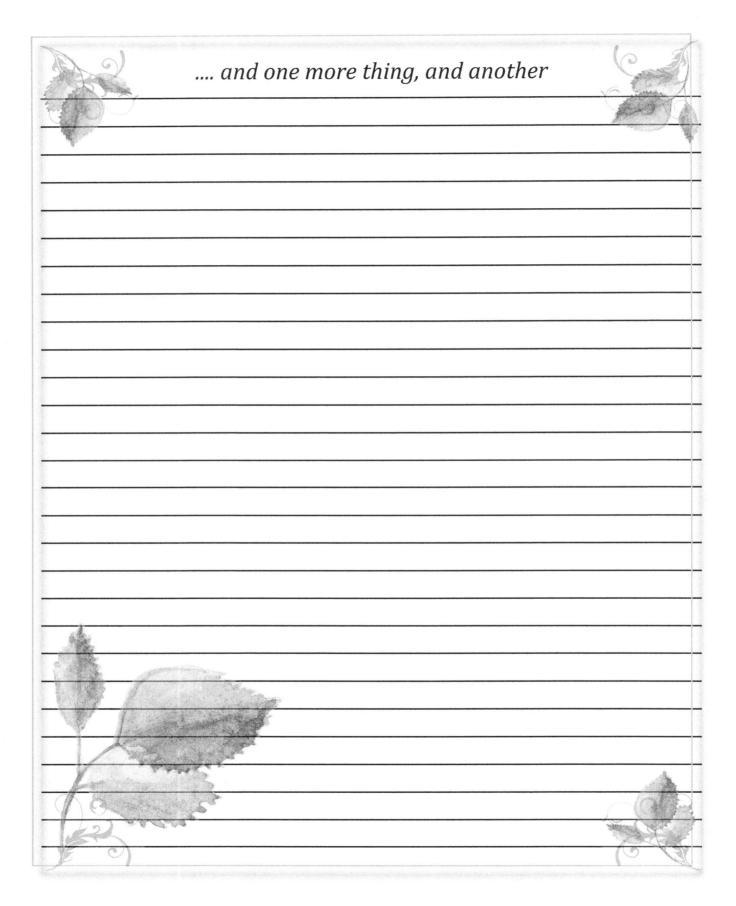

.... and one more thing, and another

APRIL
1

20

20

20

APRIL
2

$\boxed{20}$

$\boxed{20}$

$\boxed{20}$

APRIL
3

20

20

20

 # APRIL
4

(20)

(20)

(20)

APRIL
5

20

20

20

APRIL
6

(20)

(20)

(20)

APRIL
7

20

20

20

APRIL
8

(20)

(20)

(20)

APRIL
9

20

20

20

APRIL
10

$\boxed{20}$

$\boxed{20}$

$\boxed{20}$

APRIL
11

20

20

20

 # APRIL
12

20

20

20

 # APRIL

13

20

20

20

APRIL
14

20

20

20

 # APRIL

15

20

20

20

APRIL
16

20

20

20

APRIL
17

(20)

(20)

(20)

APRIL
18

20

20

20

APRIL
19

20

20

20

 # APRIL
20

(20)

(20)

(20)

APRIL
21

20

20

20

 # APRIL
22

20

20

20

APRIL
23

20

20

20

APRIL
24

20

20

20

APRIL
25

20

20

20

APRIL
26

20

20

20

 # APRIL
27

20 ⬭

20 ⬭

20 ⬭

APRIL
28

20

20

20

 # APRIL
29

20

20

20

 # APRIL
30

20

20

20

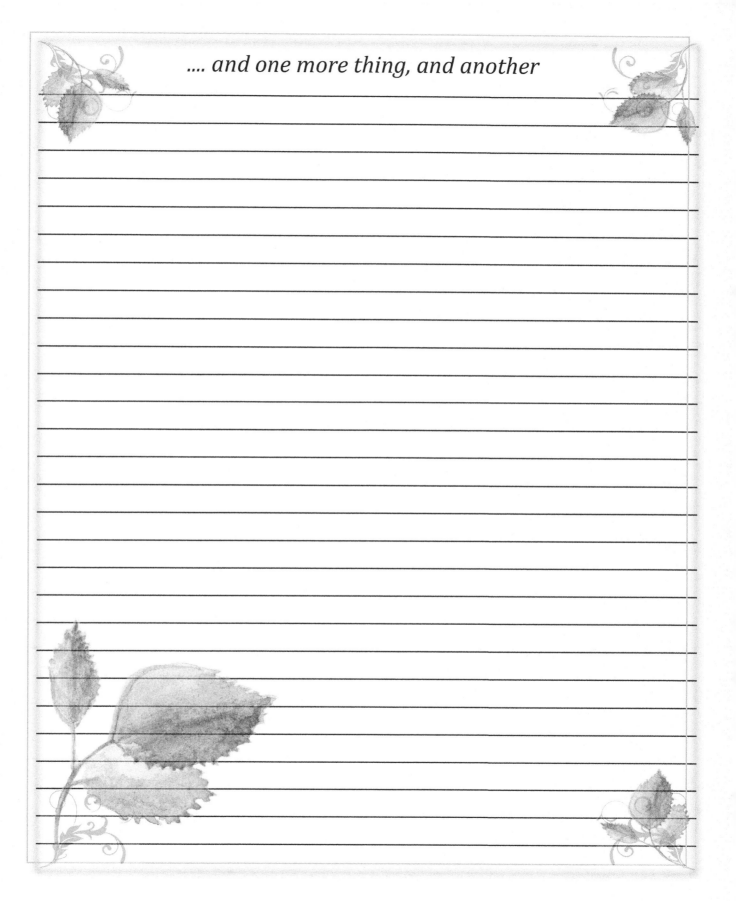

.... and one more thing, and another

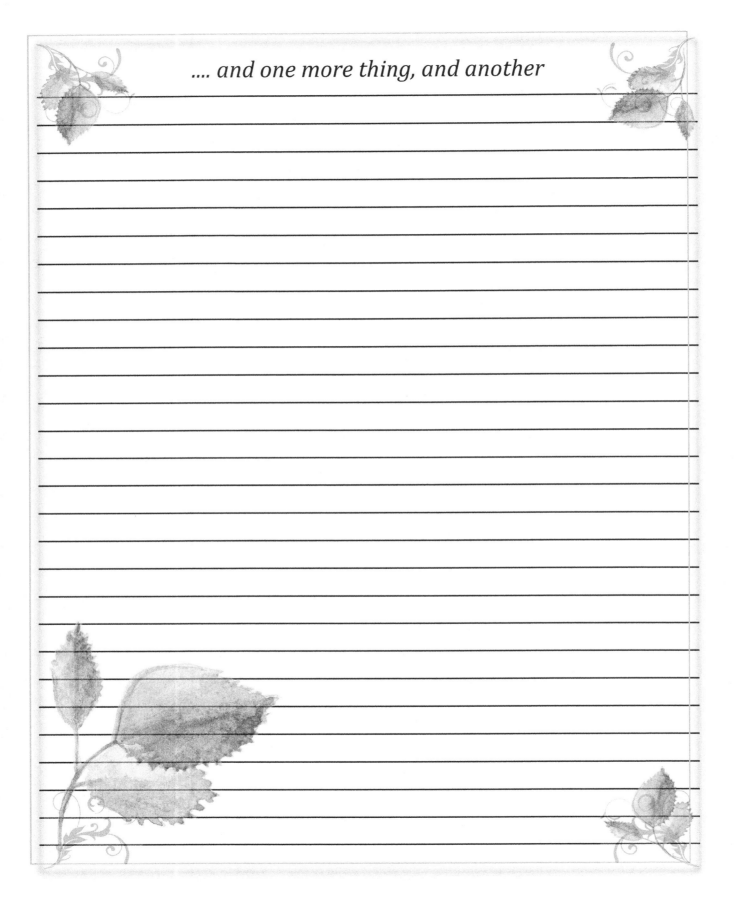

.... and one more thing, and another

MAY
1

20

20

20

 # MAY
2

(20)

(20)

(20)

 # MAY
3

20

20

20

MAY
4

20

20

20

MAY
5

20

20

20

MAY
6

$\boxed{20}$

$\boxed{20}$

$\boxed{20}$

MAY
7

20

20

20

MAY
8

20

20

20

MAY
9

20

20

20

MAY
10

$\left(\begin{array}{c} 20 \end{array}\right)$

$\left(\begin{array}{c} 20 \end{array}\right)$

$\left(\begin{array}{c} 20 \end{array}\right)$

MAY
11

20

20

20

MAY
12

(20)

(20)

(20)

MAY
13

(20)

(20)

(20)

MAY
14

(20)

(20)

(20)

MAY
15

20

20

20

MAY
16

(20)

(20)

(20)

MAY
17

20

20

20

 # MAY
18

20

20

20

MAY
19

20

20

20

MAY
20

20

20

20

MAY
21

20

20

20

MAY
22

$\left(\, 20 \,\right)$

$\left(\, 20 \,\right)$

$\left(\, 20 \,\right)$

 # MAY
23

20

20

20

MAY
24

$\left(\,20\,\right)$

$\left(\,20\,\right)$

$\left(\,20\,\right)$

MAY
25

20

20

20

MAY
26

20

20

20

MAY
27

20

20

20

 # MAY
28

20

20

20

MAY
29

20

20

20

MAY
30

$\boxed{20}$

$\boxed{20}$

$\boxed{20}$

MAY
31

20

20

20

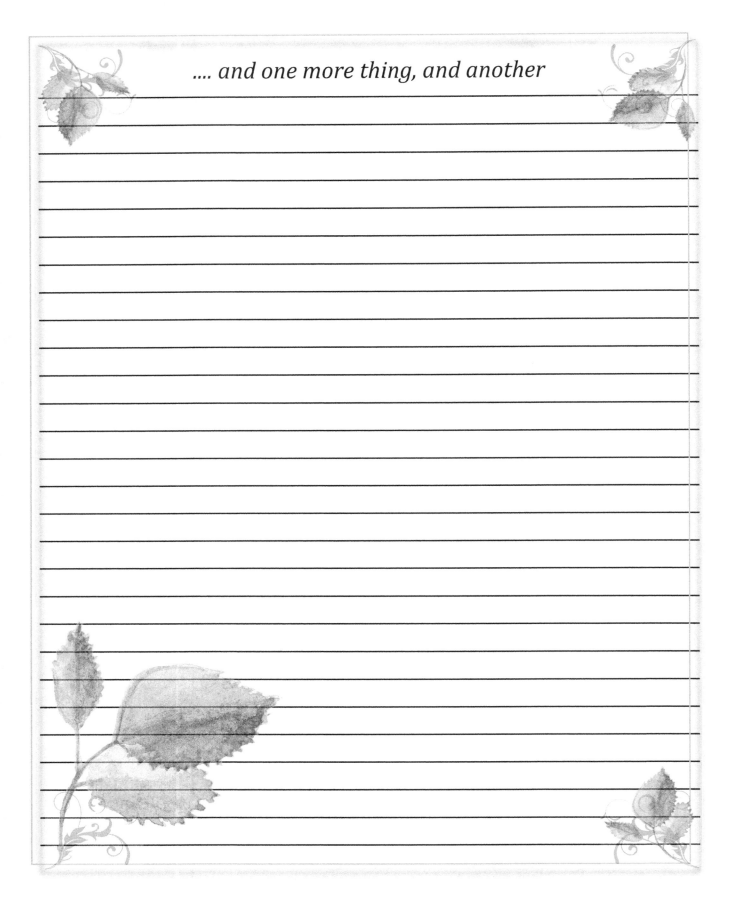

.... and one more thing, and another

.... and one more thing, and another

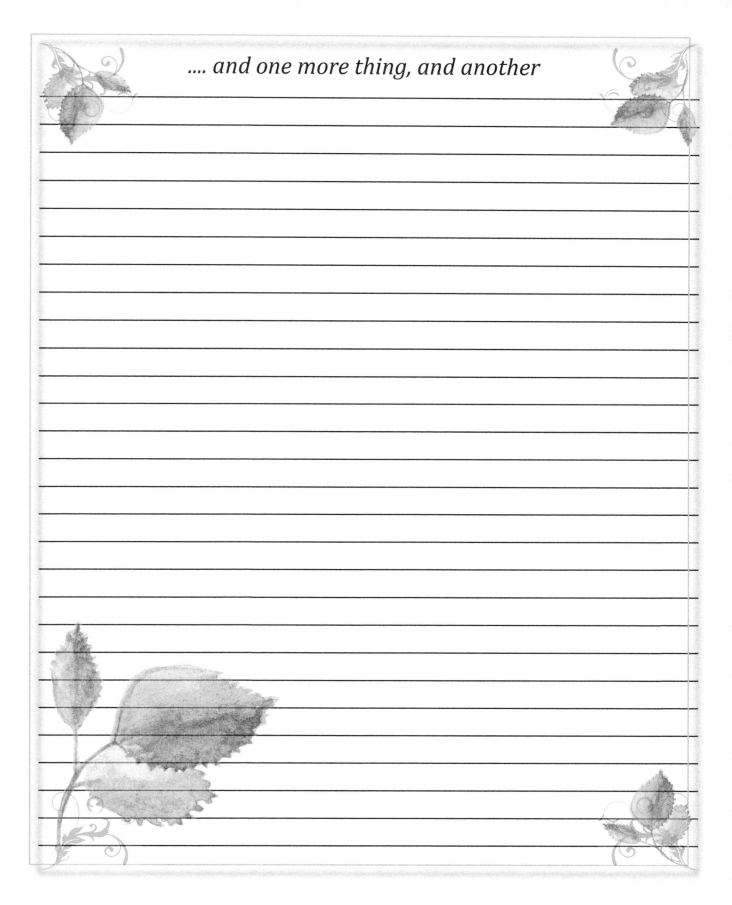

.... and one more thing, and another

 # JUNE
1

20

20

20

JUNE
2

$\boxed{20}$

$\boxed{20}$

$\boxed{20}$

JUNE
3

20

20

20

JUNE
4

$\left(\text{20}\right)$

$\left(\text{20}\right)$

$\left(\text{20}\right)$

JUNE
5

20

20

20

JUNE
6

20

20

20

JUNE
7

20

20

20

JUNE
8

20

20

20

JUNE
9

20

20

20

JUNE
10

$\bigcirc$ 20

$\bigcirc$ 20

$\bigcirc$ 20

JUNE
11

20

20

20

JUNE
12

(20)

(20)

(20)

 # JUNE
13

20

20

20

 # JUNE
14

(20)

(20)

(20)

 # JUNE
15

20

20

20

JUNE
16

20

20

20

JUNE
17

20

20

20

JUNE
18

20

20

20

JUNE
19

20

20

20

JUNE
20

20

20

20

JUNE
21

(20)

(20)

(20)

JUNE
22

20

20

20

 # JUNE
23

(20)

(20)

(20)

JUNE
24

(20)

(20)

(20)

JUNE
25

20

20

20

JUNE
26

20

20

20

JUNE
27

20

20

20

JUNE
28

20

20

20

JUNE
29

20

20

20

JUNE
30

$\boxed{20}$

$\boxed{20}$

$\boxed{20}$

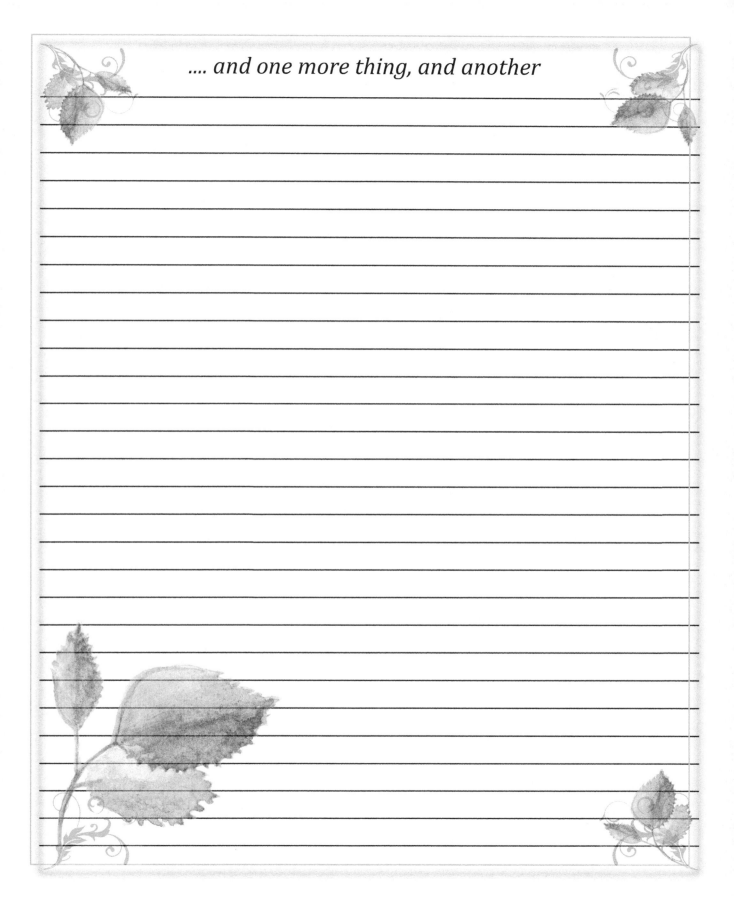

.... *and one more thing, and another*

.... and one more thing, and another

.... and one more thing, and another

.... and one more thing, and another

 # JULY

1

20

20

20

JULY
2

(20)

(20)

(20)

JULY
3

20

20

20

JULY
4

20

20

20

JULY
5

$\widehat{\quad 20 \quad}$

$\widehat{\quad 20 \quad}$

$\widehat{\quad 20 \quad}$

JULY
6

20

20

20

JULY
7

20

20

20

JULY
8

20

20

20

 # JULY
9

20

20

20

JULY
10

20

20

20

JULY
11

20

20

20

JULY
12

20 ⬯

20 ⬯

20 ⬯

JULY
13

20 ⬭

20 ⬭

20 ⬭

JULY
14

20

20

20

JULY
15

20

20

20

JULY
16

20

20

20

JULY
17

20

20

20

 # JULY
18

(20)

(20)

(20)

JULY
19

20

20

20

JULY
20

20

20

20

 # JULY
21

20

20

20

JULY
22

20

20

20

JULY
23

20 ⬭

20 ⬭

20 ⬭

 # JULY
24

20

20

20

JULY
25

20

20

20

JULY
26

20

20

20

JULY
27

20

20

20

JULY
28

(20)

(20)

(20)

JULY
29

$\boxed{20}$

$\boxed{20}$

$\boxed{20}$

JULY
30

$\left(20\quad\right)$

$\left(20\quad\right)$

$\left(20\quad\right)$

JULY
31

20

20

20

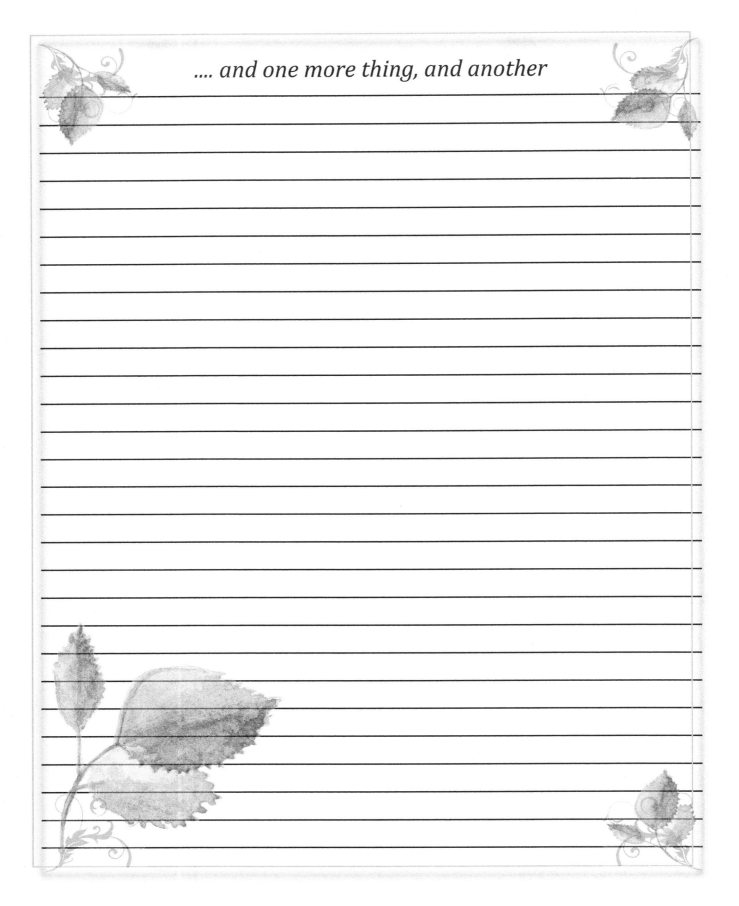

.... and one more thing, and another

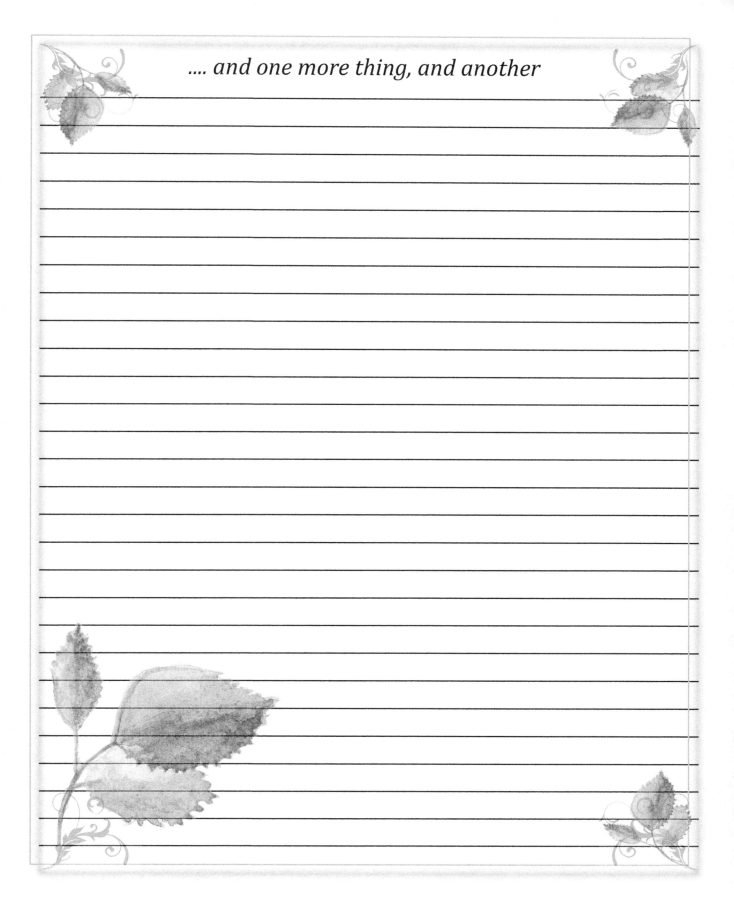

.... and one more thing, and another

.... and one more thing, and another

 # AUGUST
1

20

20

20

 # AUGUST
2

20

20

20

AUGUST
3

20

20

20

 # AUGUST
4

20

20

20

AUGUST
5

$\left(\begin{array}{c}20\end{array}\right)$

$\left(\begin{array}{c}20\end{array}\right)$

$\left(\begin{array}{c}20\end{array}\right)$

AUGUST
6

20

20

20

 # AUGUST
7

20

20

20

AUGUST

8

20

20

20

AUGUST
9

20

20

20

AUGUST
10

20

20

20

 # AUGUST
11

20

20

20

AUGUST
12

20

20

20

AUGUST
13

20⎯

20⎯

20⎯

 # AUGUST
14

20

20

20

 # AUGUST
15

20

20

20

 # AUGUST
16

(20)

(20)

(20)

 # AUGUST
17

20

20

20

 # AUGUST
18

(20)

(20)

(20)

 # AUGUST
19

20

20

20

AUGUST

20

(20)

(20)

(20)

AUGUST
21

20

20

20

 # AUGUST
22

20

20

20

AUGUST
23

20

20

20

AUGUST
24

$\left(20\right)$

$\left(20\right)$

$\left(20\right)$

AUGUST
25

20

20

20

AUGUST
26

20

20

20

 # AUGUST
27

20

20

20

AUGUST
28

20

20

20

AUGUST
29

20

20

20

 # AUGUST
30

(20)

(20)

(20)

AUGUST
31

20

20

20

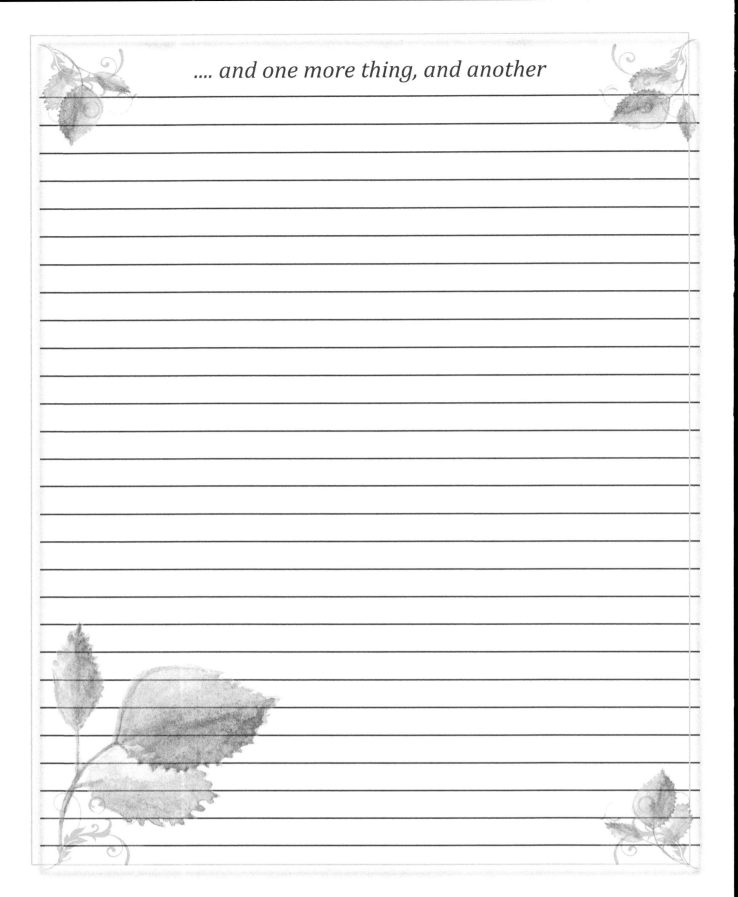

.... and one more thing, and another

.... and one more thing, and another

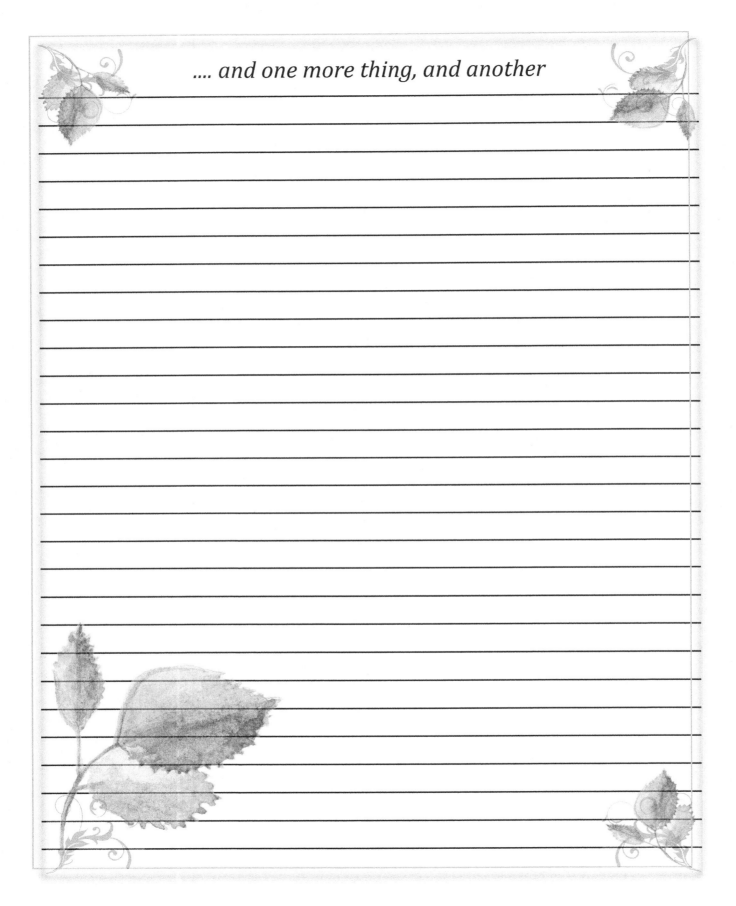

.... and one more thing, and another

SEPTEMBER
1

20

20

20

SEPTEMBER
2

20

20

20

SEPTEMBER
3

20

20

20

SEPTEMBER
4

20

20

20

 # SEPTEMBER
5

20

20

20

SEPTEMBER
6

20

20

20

 # SEPTEMBER

7

20

20

20

SEPTEMBER
8

20

20

20

 # SEPTEMBER

9

20

20

20

 # SEPTEMBER
10

20

20

20

 # SEPTEMBER

11

20

20

20

 # SEPTEMBER
12

20

20

20

 # SEPTEMBER

13

20

20

20

SEPTEMBER
14

20

20

20

 # SEPTEMBER

15

20

20

20

 # SEPTEMBER

16

20

20

20

 # SEPTEMBER
17

20

20

20

 # SEPTEMBER

18

20

20

20

SEPTEMBER
19

20

20

20

SEPTEMBER
20

20

20

20

SEPTEMBER
21

20

20

20

SEPTEMBER
22

20

20

20

SEPTEMBER
23

$\boxed{20}$

$\boxed{20}$

$\boxed{20}$

SEPTEMBER
24

20

20

20

SEPTEMBER
25

20

20

20

SEPTEMBER
26

$\left(\!20\!\right)$

$\left(\!20\!\right)$

$\left(\!20\!\right)$

 # SEPTEMBER
27

20

20

20

 # SEPTEMBER
28

20

20

20

SEPTEMBER
29

20

20

20

 # SEPTEMBER
30

20

20

20

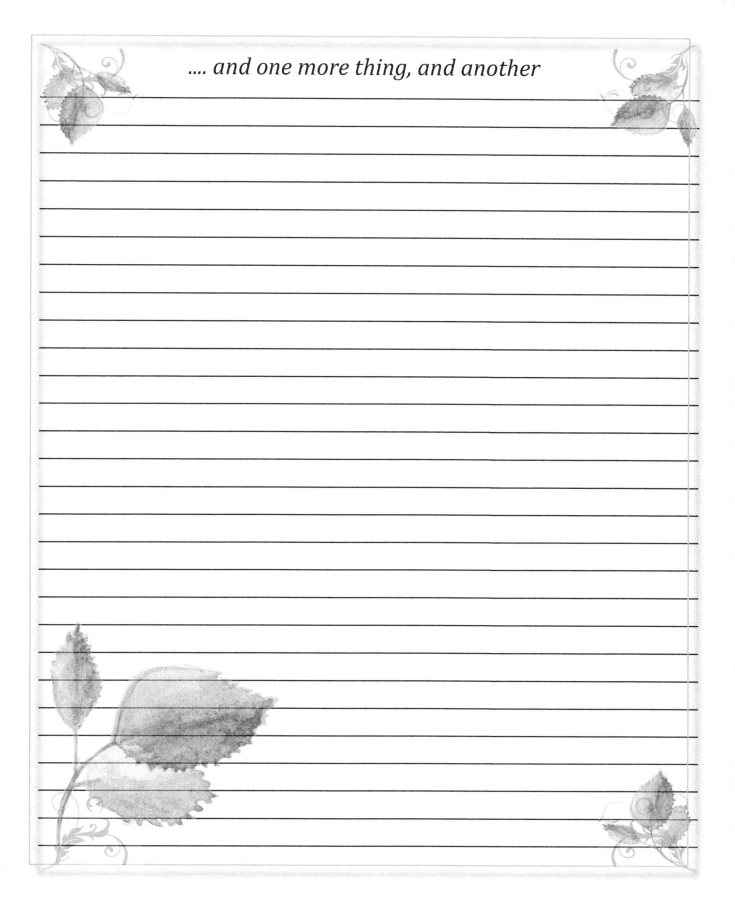

.... and one more thing, and another

.... and one more thing, and another

OCTOBER
1

20

20

20

 # OCTOBER
2

20

20

20

 # OCTOBER
3

20

20

20

 # OCTOBER

4

20

20

20

 # OCTOBER

5

(20)

(20)

(20)

OCTOBER
6

20

20

20

OCTOBER
7

20

20

20

 # OCTOBER
8

20

20

20

 # OCTOBER
9

20

20

20

 # OCTOBER
10

20

20

20

 # OCTOBER

11

20

20

20

 # OCTOBER

12

20

20

20

 # OCTOBER
13

20

20

20

 # OCTOBER
14

20

20

20

OCTOBER
15

20

20

20

 # OCTOBER
16

20

20

20

 # OCTOBER

17

$\widehat{20}$

$\widehat{20}$

$\widehat{20}$

 # OCTOBER
18

20

20

20

 # OCTOBER

19

20

20

20

 # OCTOBER
20

20

20

Mom's One Line a Day by Diana Lynn Copyright © 2018 D &D Graphics

 # OCTOBER
21

20

20

20

# OCTOBER
22

20

20

20

OCTOBER
23

$\big(\,20\,\big)$

$\big(\,20\,\big)$

$\big(\,20\,\big)$

 # OCTOBER
24

20

20

20

 # OCTOBER
25

20

20

20

 # OCTOBER

26

20

20

20

OCTOBER
27

20

20

20

 # OCTOBER
28

20

20

20

 # OCTOBER
29

(20)

(20)

(20)

OCTOBER
30

20

20

20

 # OCTOBER
31

20

20

20

.... and one more thing, and another

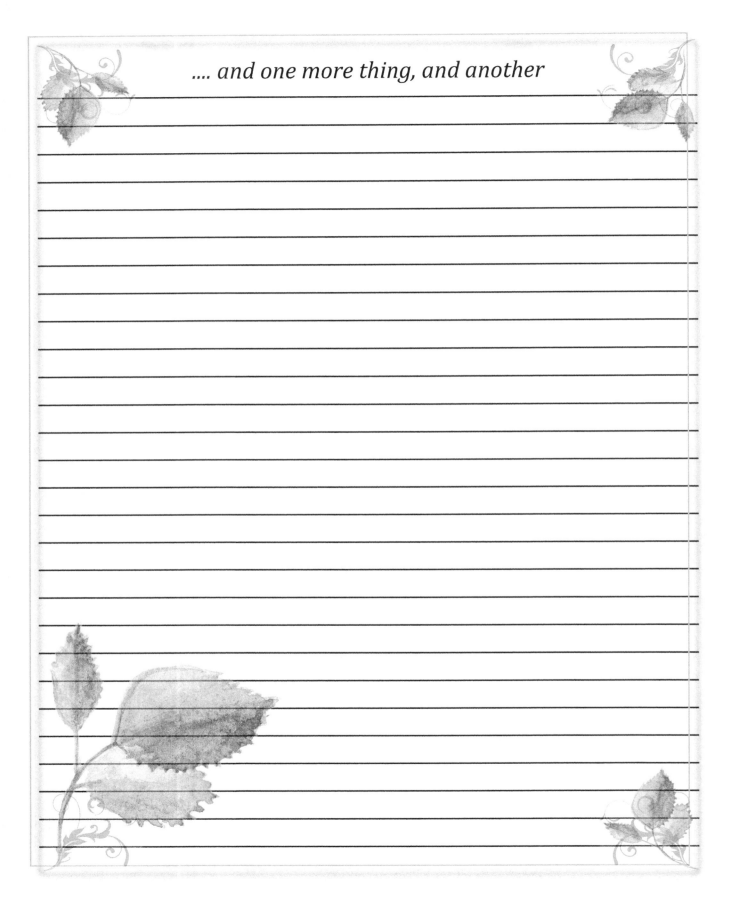

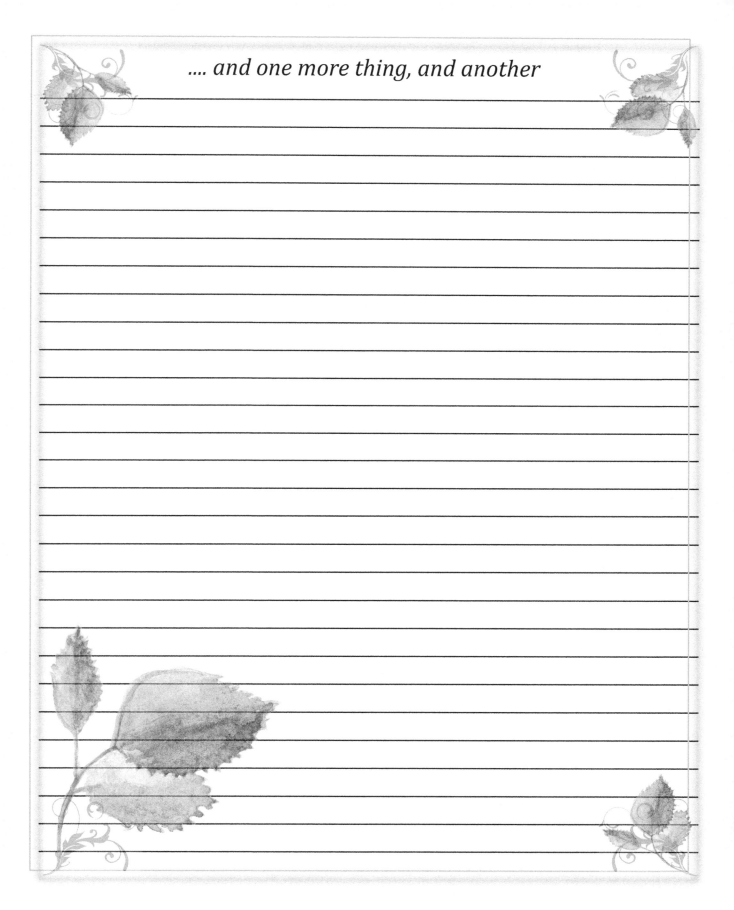

.... *and one more thing, and another*

.... and one more thing, and another

 # NOVEMBER

1

20

20

20

 # NOVEMBER
2

20

20

20

 # NOVEMBER
3

20

20

20

NOVEMBER
4

20

20

20

 # NOVEMBER
5

20

20

20

NOVEMBER
6

20

20

20

 # NOVEMBER
7

20

20

20

NOVEMBER
8

20

20

20

NOVEMBER
9

(20)

(20)

(20)

 # NOVEMBER
10

(20)

(20)

(20)

NOVEMBER
11

20

20

20

 # NOVEMBER
12

(20)

(20)

(20)

 # NOVEMBER

13

20

20

20

 # NOVEMBER
14

20

20

20

 # NOVEMBER
15

(20)

(20)

(20)

 # NOVEMBER

16

$\left(\text{20}\quad\right)$

$\left(\text{20}\quad\right)$

$\left(\text{20}\quad\right)$

 # NOVEMBER
17

$\left(\begin{array}{c}20\end{array}\right)$

$\left(\begin{array}{c}20\end{array}\right)$

$\left(\begin{array}{c}20\end{array}\right)$

 # NOVEMBER

18

$\boxed{20}$

$\boxed{20}$

$\boxed{20}$

 # NOVEMBER

19

$\left(\ 20\ \right)$

$\left(\ 20\ \right)$

$\left(\ 20\ \right)$

NOVEMBER

20

20

20

# NOVEMBER
21

20

20

20

NOVEMBER
22

20

20

20

 # NOVEMBER
23

 # NOVEMBER
24

$\left(\begin{array}{c} 20 \end{array}\right)$

$\left(\begin{array}{c} 20 \end{array}\right)$

$\left(\begin{array}{c} 20 \end{array}\right)$

 # NOVEMBER
25

$\boxed{20}$

$\boxed{20}$

$\boxed{20}$

 # NOVEMBER
26

(20)

(20)

(20)

 # NOVEMBER
27

NOVEMBER
28

20

20

20

NOVEMBER
29

20

20

20

NOVEMBER 30

(20)

(20)

(20)

.... and one more thing, and another

.... and one more thing, and another

 # DECEMBER

1

20

20

20

 # DECEMBER

2

20

20

20

 # DECEMBER

3

20

20

20

 # DECEMBER
4

20

20

20

 # DECEMBER
5

20

20

20

 # DECEMBER

6

20

20

20

 # DECEMBER
7

(20)

(20)

(20)

 # DECEMBER
8

(20)

(20)

(20)

DECEMBER
9

20

20

20

 # DECEMBER

10

$\boxed{20}$

$\boxed{20}$

$\boxed{20}$

DECEMBER
11

$\left(20\right)$

$\left(20\right)$

$\left(20\right)$

DECEMBER
12

20

20

20

DECEMBER
13

20

20

20

 # DECEMBER

14

20

20

20

 # DECEMBER
15

20

20

20

 # DECEMBER

16

20

20

20

 # DECEMBER

17

20

20

20

 # DECEMBER

18

20

20

20

 # DECEMBER
19

20

20

20

# DECEMBER
20

20

20

20

 # DECEMBER

21

20

20

20

 # DECEMBER
22

20

20

20

 # DECEMBER
23

20

20

20

DECEMBER
24

20

20

20

DECEMBER
25

20

20

20

 # DECEMBER
26

20

20

20

 # DECEMBER
27

20

20

20

 # DECEMBER

28

(20)

(20)

(20)

 # DECEMBER
29

20

20

20

 # DECEMBER
30

20

20

20

DECEMBER
31

$\boxed{20}$

$\boxed{20}$

$\boxed{20}$

.... and one more thing, and another

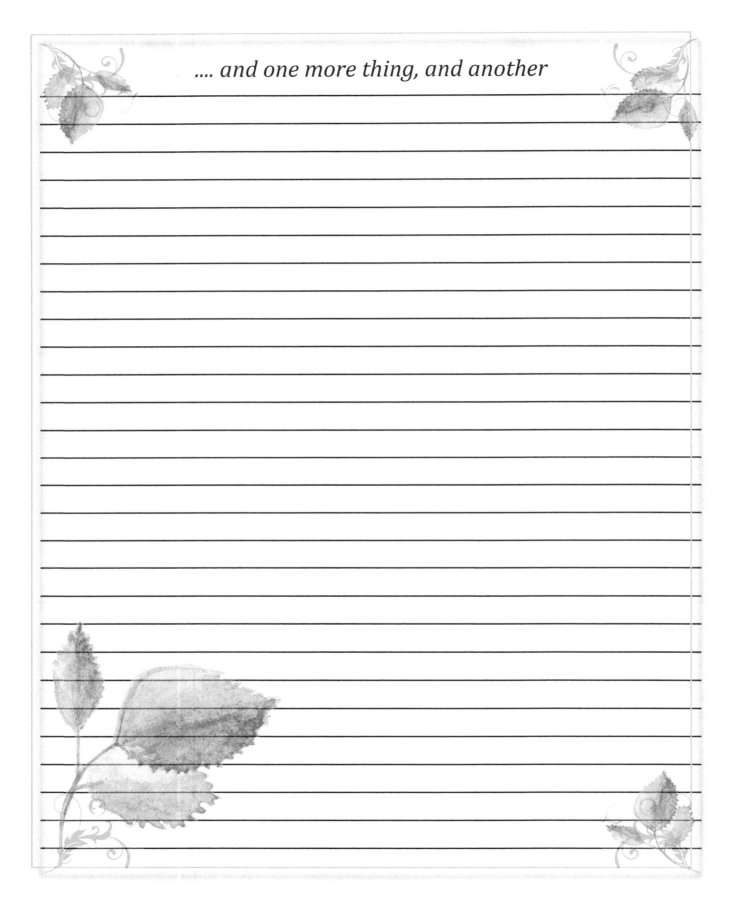

.... and one more thing, and another

.... and one more thing, and another

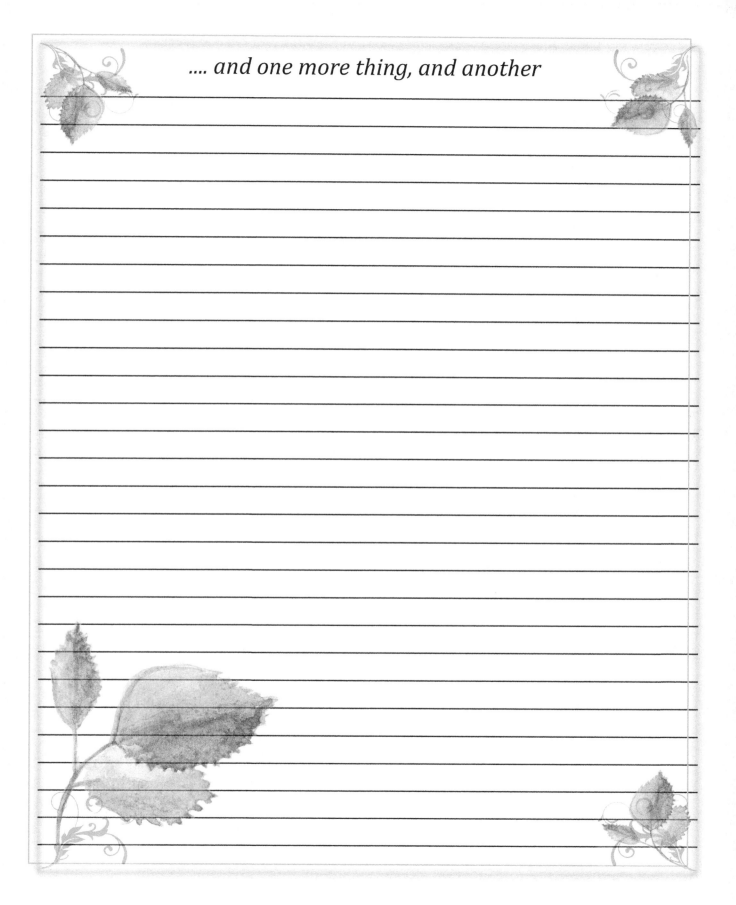

.... and one more thing, and another

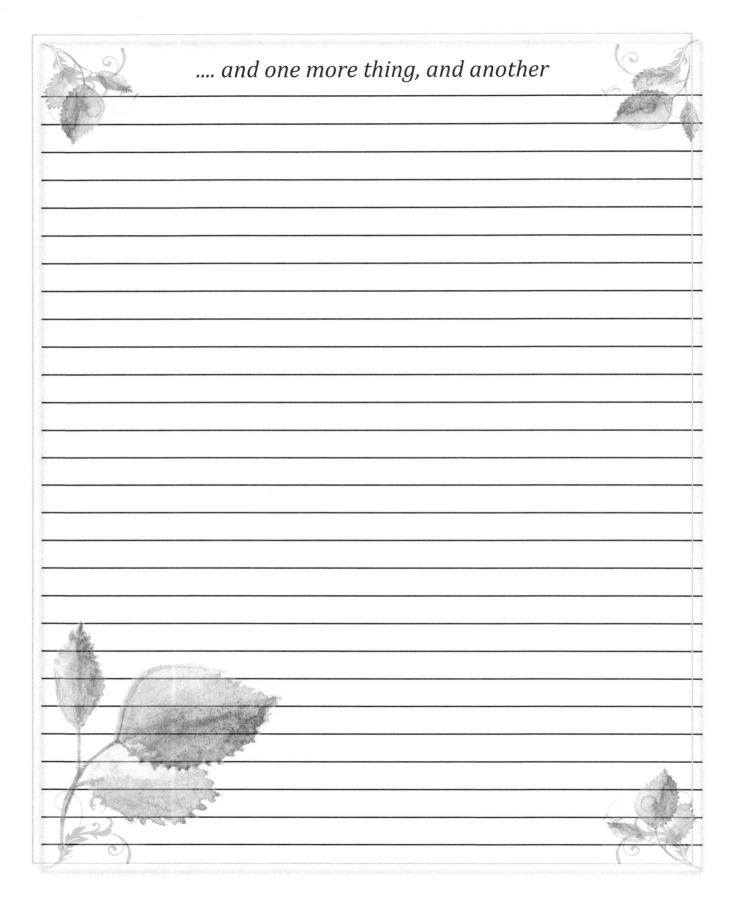

.... and one more thing, and another

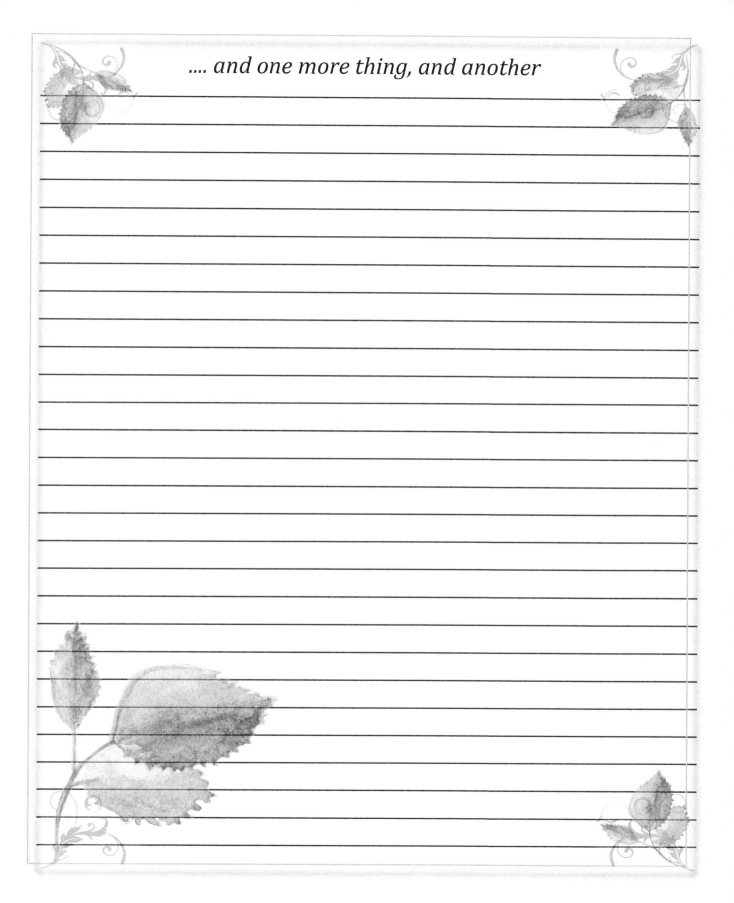

.... and one more thing, and another

ISBN 978-1-947594-01-2

Published by D&D Graphics in 2018
First edition; First printing

Made in United States
Orlando, FL
10 December 2021

11460301R00226